To Marje & Todd

Enjoy!

Matthias Breiter

Matthias Breiter
Denali Nat. Park
August 19th 2017

BreiterView Publishing

DENALI

Crown Jewel of America

Matthias Breiter

BreiterView Publishing

To Aislyn, Kiri & Aneira

Acknowledgements

I am deeply indebted to all my friends in Alaska, particularly to Jim Trumbull, Todd Hardesty, Deborah Schildt and Murray Bartholomew, Krista Stearns, Mona Lidgard, Mark Newman, Tony Dawson, Gary Schultz, Kim Heacox, Craig Brandt, and Terri Bernard. Without them, many photographic trips would have been impossible. Eric Matheson undertook the task to edit the manuscript. Many more have helped me over the years. I hope they will forgive me that their name was omitted due to space constraints or my forgetfulness.

Above all I am indebted to my wife Laurel Snyder, who is a limitless source of encouragement and patience, even when I again depart for a prolonged trip to photograph in Denali. And last but not least I am thankful to my daughters Aislyn, Kiri and Aneira. All three supported me with their smiles and cheerful dispositions during the long hours of designing the book.

Matthias Breiter
Kenora, Ontario, March 2017

page 1: Sunset on Denali from Petersville
page 2-3: Denali and Mount Hunter or Begguya
page 5-6: Moose bull in Igloo forest
page 7-8: Aurora borealis over Denali and Mount Foraker or Sultana

Book Marks

DENALI - BEACON OF THE WILD

Soft moonlight illuminates Denali in autumn

> *"In wilderness I sense the miracle of life, and behind it our scientific accomplishments fade to trivia."*
>
> Charles Lindbergh

Moose bull in Wonder Lake ▶

The rain has stopped. The land sparkles clean. The air smells fresh as if the world is reborn. Mist shrouds the hillsides in a white, undulating tunic, a living blanket revealing ravines as the cloth is drawn away while hiding others where the fog thickens. A male caribou adorned with huge antlers still wrapped in velvet passes by, ignoring my presence. He seems to float across the tundra, his leg tendons clicking softly in the rhythm of his graceful gate. The call of a song sparrow cuts clear through the stillness of the evening. The rolling hills are cast in a warm, diffuse light neither night nor day. On the southern horizon, the lower slopes of the Alaska Range lose themselves in the clouds above. There is a peacefulness to this land, a nobility that penetrates one's soul. When I first soaked up the sounds, smell and sights of this sprawling land, I felt like I had arrived home, a sensation that has remained ever since.

Sitting on a rise, I watch as the clouds slowly lift. Rocky ridges, steep slopes and mountain walls emerge. Summits appear, cloaked in ice and snow. Finally the last veil is pulled back. Denali towers in sudden nakedness above the vastness of central Alaska, its giant mass bathed in hues of pink cast by the midnight sun. The mountain defies our concept of greatness and size. It overwhelms one's senses. It draws one close, mesmerizes, casts its spell, demands reverence and respect, and repels and punishes those that approach wanting in both. At 20,310 feet (6,190 m) Denali is the tallest peak in North America. However, measurements and numbers fade and become almost insignificant in its presence. Denali has to be experienced and felt. The mountain is an unchallenged king, a giant among its own kind. Today it reigns tall over one of the greatest protected areas in the world: Denali National Park & Preserve, the crown jewel of America.

Visually, Denali dominates the park. The protected area encompasses in total just over 6 million acres (9,492 sq mi, 24,584 sq km) and is larger than the state of New Hampshire. In circumference it measures 606 miles (975 km). A crow would need to fly 130 miles in a straight line to cross the park east to west and only slightly less north to south. Yet, from a vantage point, the mountain looms tall against the sky even from the furthest corners of the park. However, despite its visual prominence, the park was created to safeguard a threatened ecosystem. As a matter of fact, it was the first national park explicitly established to protect wildlife. That it contained within its boundaries the highest summit in the United States was coincidental and helpful in the campaign for its creation.

On February 26, 1917, when President Wilson signed the bill into legislation, Mount McKinley National Park, as the protected area was initially known, become the 13th national park of the United States. The summit of Denali, ironically, was not within the newly created park, which was remedied in 1922 when the boundaries were first adjusted to reflect habitat use of wildlife populations. Since then, the park was enlarged twice more and in 1980 renamed Denali National Park and Preserve covering now almost four times its original size.

Already in 1976, the park was designated an International Biosphere Reserve in recognition of its value as a conservation area. This subarctic wilderness contains over 1500 species of plants. 39 species of mammals, 169 species of birds, most of them migrants, and one

amphibian, the wood frog. Denali has been aptly dubbed "Serengeti of the North".

Over 500 000 visitors arrive annually in the park. Most want to see the big five: grizzly, moose, Dall sheep, caribou, wolf, and, in addition, possibly above all, Denali itself. However, Denali is more than an accumulation of its wild denizens towered over by a lofty peak. Denali is a beacon of the wild, a reminder of wilderness values, a place were we are still able to appreciate nature in its unaltered form. It is a place that encourages us to slow down, escape from the vexes of modern life and immerse ourselves in a world where time seems to stand still.

The corniced summits of Mount Church, Mount Grosvenor, Mount Johnson and Mount Bradley stand sentinel over the Great Gorge of the Ruth Glacier. ▲

Above the deeply crevassed glacier in the Don Sheldon Amphitheater , the East Buttress leads up to Denali's south summit. It takes climbers up to three weeks to scale the seven mile long ridge. ▶

Both caribou and grizzly make their home in Denali. The bears generally pay little attention to the herbivore. Vice versa, caribou usually behave indifferently and display nonchalance toward the massive predator, even if they are near by. A healthy adult caribou can easily outrun a grizzly. Even a calf more than two weeks old is generally too fleet-footed for the bear to catch. However, the bruins are the ultimate opportunist and quick to pick up on injured or sick individuals.

Moose are the largest member of the deer family, and some of the biggest individuals in the world can be found in Denali. A bull in prime condition may weigh in at 1,600 pounds (725 kg) and can stand 6.9 feet at the shoulder (2.1 m). Their antlers reach their largest size when the animals are 10-12 years old. A huge bull may grow a rack weighing 80 pounds (36.3 kg) over the course of the summer, adding a pound of bone a day. The tips of their tines on opposite sides of their head may be well over 60 inches (152 cm) apart.

Bulls often spend their summers in small bachelor groups on the hillsides. Many females, by contrast, especially if they are with calf, stay at lower elevation in the forest zone where they stand a better chance to protect their offspring from predators. Only in the fall do bulls and cows abandon their segregated lifestyle and congregate in rutting areas.

Denali looms above valleys smothered in fog in the fall.

A brilliant autumn sunrise over the Alaska Range near Sanctuary River.

In fall, the tundra is set ablaze when willow and blue berry bushes turn crimson. It is one of nature's most splendid displays, yet as with so many things in this northern environment, also fleeting. As the days get shorter and temperatures drop, so do the colorful leaves. Soon, snow will cover the land and protect the bare branches underneath its white mantel from the bitter cold.

Aspen, poplar and birch trees add a touch of yellow and orange to the taiga forest in the park entrance area.

The trunks of balsam poplar and quaking aspen reach for the winter sky.

Oblivious to the dramatic scenery, a mixed group of Dall sheep including ewes, lambs and a large ram feed up high on Primrose Ridge.

The sun breaking through the clouds casts a spot light on a group of Dall sheep on a high mountain meadow.

Denali delights in vastness. It is a place in size often too large to attach scale. Amidst the enormity of the landscape, it is easy to seek beauty only in its grandness, in the obvious and when conditions are perfect. Yet nature's artistry can also be found in the small, the unassuming, the inconspicuous, when clouds hang low, when drizzle wets the tundra, and when frost stiffens ones joints. Wandering with open eyes and an inquisitive mind, unforgettable memories are made on every journey into the park regardless of weather and season.

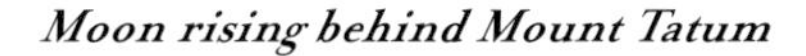

Moon rising behind Mount Tatum

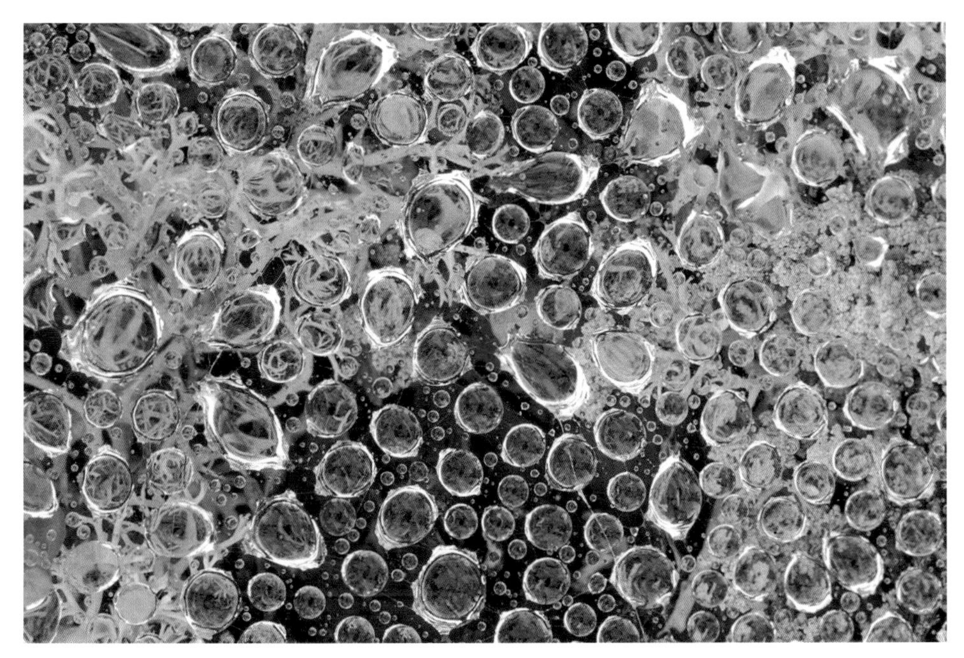

Dew drops on a spider web woven above lichen.

Frost crystals rimming the leaves of bunchberry plants.

It is hidden in ancient prehistory when the first people crossed from Asia to North America via the Bering land bridge. Archaeological evidence suggest that they came at least 15,000 years ago. Remains within the park have been dated to be over 12,000 years old. These ice-age migrants would have come for the abundant wildlife. Yet undoubtedly they would also have gazed in awe at the mountain towering above them. And countless generations ago, these ancestors of the Koyukon Athabaskans began to refer to the mountain as "Denali", "the Great One". In essence, the appeal of the region is timeless and crosses cultural and economic boundaries.

By comparison, the history of people with European ancestry in the region occurred within the blink of an eye. Precisely when they first set eyes on the mountain is unknown. In all likelihood it was Russian fur traders venturing up along the coast. However, they left no written record of their discoveries. On May 25, 1778, Captain James Cook aboard the HMS Resolution entered Cook Inlet. Cook was meticulous in describing every detail of the land he "discovered". Yet, as there is no entry in his log book mentioning large mountains on the northern horizon, clouds may have obscured them. George Vancouver was a member of the Cook expedition in 1778. Sixteen years later he was put in charge of a new expedition along the Pacific Coast and returned to Cook Inlet aboard the 99ft sloop "Discovery". His orders were to survey the coast and, if it so happens, find the Northwest Passage. The latter he did not, beyond proving that no such seaway existed at the latitude suggested. However, his charts proved to be so exceedingly accurate that they served as key reference for coastal navigation for generations. But Vancouver did more than survey the coastline. While in Knik Arm, north of present day Anchorage, he noted on May 6 in his logbook the sighting of "distant stupendous mountains", the first known written record of Denali.

Over the next one hundred years, few non-natives

Autumn sunrise on Denali ▶

FIRST ENCOUNTERS

visited the Denali area. Most of Alaska, except for coastal areas and major river corridors, remained unexplored. In 1867, the United States bought Alaska from Russia. The Russian Crown was in desperate need of funds and Russian America had lost its economic value as the fur trade had largely collapsed due to over-harvesting. Soon after the transfer of title, gold was found along the Stikine River. A few years later, more discoveries followed further north. Successive stampedes washed prospectors into Alaska and the Yukon territory. In their search of Eldorado, they went where no white men had gone before, staking claims in a land that was essentially unknown to the government. It became a necessity to survey Alaska and provide detailed maps. By the late 1890s, the United States Geological Survey began to send geologic and topographic field parties into many of the remote areas of Alaska. Finally, in 1902, an exploratory trip led by Alfred H. Brooks, the head of the Alaskan branch of the USGS left Cook Inlet, traversed the Alaska Range and travelled along its northwest flank through what is now Denali National Park to the Nenana River. Many of the prominent geographic features of the park were named during this expedition including Peters Glacier and Peters Dome, Muldrow Glacier and Mount Brooks. The expedition provided the first topographic maps of the area. But Brooks was not blind to the area's diverse and abundant wildlife. He noted that "on the north slopes of the mountains, moose, caribou, and mountain sheep, or big horns, were unusually plentiful ... the party was never without fresh meat."

A year later, the first climbing parties arrived. While they were unsuccessful in conquering the mountain, they too noted the great number of game animals. The adventurer Dr. Frederick Cook, leader of an East Coast climbing party, wrote: "Here along the northern slope of the McKinley ground, we crossed the best game country in America. Caribou, moose, mountain sheep, and grizzly bears were constantly in evidence." Judge James Wickersham, member of a group of hopeful mountaineers from Fairbanks, declared the area "a hunter's paradise". He

The setting sun illuminates clouds above the Alaska Range. ▲

Evening light on Denali and Mount Hunter, also known as Begguya, meaning "Child".

Alpenglow on Mount Brooks

even suggested to protect the region within a scenic land withdrawal, a highly unusual move at the time by one of the most powerful and influential people in Alaska.

In 1906, Charles Sheldon arrived in what is now Denali National Park. He came to study Dall sheep, but soon realized a summer spent afield was simply not enough to do the animal and area justice. He thus returned in 1907 and overwintered in a cabin he built with the help of Harry Karstens on the Toklat River, a few miles downstream from where the bridge of the park road is located today. Sheldon's interests quickly grew beyond the study of Dall sheep to include other mammals as well as birds and plants. An idea, which became a conviction and passion, formed in his mind. In his diary he notes that because of the "beauties of the country and of the variety of the game," the area "would make an ideal park and game preserve." He antici-

Caribou bull in front of Wickersham Wall

pated the "enjoyment and inspiration visitors will receive" from this area. The need for a protected area became clearly evident when he encountered camps of market hunters in the Savage, Sanctuary, Teklanika and Toklat river valleys. They supplied meat to the boom city of Fairbanks and gold rush towns such as Kantishna. Sheldon was particularly appalled that half if not more of the meat harvested was used to feed the dog teams and never even made it to its destination.

Shortly after he returned to New York in January

Tundra at Thorofare Pass ▲

Wolverine ◀

Moose bull passing in front of Denali ▶

1909, Sheldon pitched the idea of a wildlife preserve. Although among his peers his idea was greeted enthusiastically, it gained little political support initially. Conservation was not a top priority for the new administration in Washington. Instead there was a push for further development of Alaska. On March 12, 1914, Congress passed the Alaska Railroad Act, which provided funding to build the rail line from Seward to Fairbanks. Sheldon quickly realized that improved access to the Denali region would in all likelihood result in the demise of the local wildlife populations. With new urgency, he again began to lobby for the creation of a protected area. And he succeeded. On February 26, 1917, the region was put under permanent protection for present and future generations to enjoy. Mount McKinley National Park was born. Enlarged several times and renamed in 1980 as Denali National Park and Preserve, it is one of the greatest natural treasures in America.

The protection of wildlife, especially of Dall sheep, was the reason for the establishment of the park. The animals are still prevalent in Denali. They are often observed as white dots high up on a mountain side, easily mistaken for dirty specks of snow. About 2,500 individuals live on the north side of the Alaska Range. Numbers have fluctuated greatly over the years. Particularly unfavorable winter conditions take their toll and decades may pass until the populations rebound.

A band of Dall sheep on Sable Mountain ▶

Denali as seen from Sable Pass

"Let us be guardians, not gardeners."

Adolph Murie

The Teklanika River Valley

Weather in Denali is unpredictable. Snow can fall any month of the year. Occasionally, on hot summer days, violent thunderstorms move in, gales tug on tent guy lines, heavy rain drenches the land and hours later the tundra swelters under the sun again. Backpackers novice to the Far North often fail to appreciate that at a high latitude the rays of the sun carry a punch. Overexposure to ultraviolet radiation often goes unnoticed in the pleasant ambient temperatures. As a consequence, badly burned skin has dampened the spirit of many hikers. On the open tundra there is no shade to get out of the sun, and the nights are short.

Storm clouds unload heavy rain over the hills west of the Teklanika River.

The day dawns clear in Anchorage. Not a cloud obscures the sky. Long before the sun climbs across the Chugach Mountains and drives the chill of morning away, it illuminates the majestic summits on the northern horizon. The mountains seem to blush in the embrace of the warming rays. Denali and its companion Sultana, as Mt. Foraker is locally known, appear like a glistening mirage. Too large to be true. The summit is 140 miles (225 km) distant yet clearly visible, tempting, alluring. By car it is 115 miles (185 km) to Talkeetna, the gateway to the mountain for climbers, and 135 miles (217 km) to the South Overlook, a two to three hour leisurely drive. For much of the way, the road appears to lead to the mountain's very feet. The easy approach via pavement or railroad tracks is deceiving. Before the road was built and the tracks laid, a journey to reach Denali's base from the south was arduous to say the least, and any attempt almost inevitably failed. The mountain seemed to beckon, yet the land re-

Approach from The South

pelled the ambitious traveler. The Alaska Range is a moisture and temperature barrier. North of its divide, a dry continental climate prevails with temperatures dipping in winter to as far as 50 below Fahrenheit if not colder. Little snow falls. Summers are hot and thunderstorms common. On the south side, temperatures are vastly more moderate. Summers are cool and moist. Nature thrives in the mild conditions and life explodes under the long daylight hours. Salmon travel up the Susitna River where bears and eagles claim their bounty. At lower elevation, along the streams, dense stands of cottonwood and poplar form a lofty canopy above a veritable jungle of devil's club and alders. The thickets are next to impenetrable. Heavy precipitation transforms rivers and streams into violent torrents dangerous to cross. In winter, snow devours the land, submerging it under an insulating blanket so deep that even long-legged moose struggle to fight through. The ice skinning lake and stream surfaces is often treacherous, rendering

Mount Foraker peeking shyly from behind the Tokosha Mountains covered in fresh snow. According to Hudson Stuck, who led the first ascent of Denali, the natives had two names for Mount Foraker: Sultana meaning "the woman" and Menlale meaning "Denali's wife".

crossings a risky, unsafe endeavor. Not surprisingly, during the early days of exploration, all successful expeditions to reach the mountain where made from the north, very often using dog teams. As the road climbs from lowland river bottoms to Alpine tundra, traversing Denali State Park and brushing up to the national park boundary along its route, superb views escort the drive north. Today, we can enjoy the lushness and scenic beauty the southern approach offers unimpeded and mostly unaware that the natural splendor used to come at a price to travelers.

Sunrise on Denali from along the Petersville Road.

New green drapes the bushes and trees on a glorious spring day on the south side of the Alaska Range.

During the summer months, clear views of Denali are few and far between. Clouds often linger around the mountain's base. Frequently light rain falls. The high precipitation supports lush growth including cow parsnip or pushki. Its umbrella of tiny white flowers provides a stage for the presentation of a sparrow. Pushki is an important traditional food plant as it has edible marrow and roots that are rich in sugar and taste much like licorice. However, cow parsnip comes with a catch. Chemicals in its sap and outer hairs can cause skin irritation and, when exposed to ultraviolet radiation, severe sun burns.

The distance swallows scale. At 14,573 feet (4,442 m), Mount Hunter is more than twice as tall as the Tokosha Mountains in the foreground.

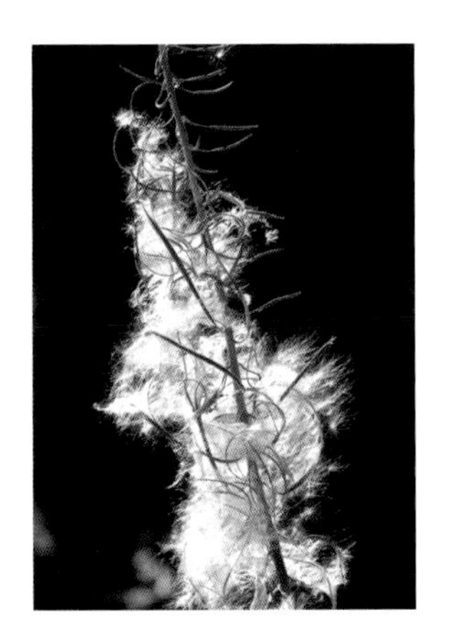

Fireweed lines the road from Anchorage to Denali. The flower is the unofficial Alaskan calendar plant. It blooms sequentially from the bottom towards the top over the course of the summer. When the wind finally carries the fluffy seeds to new ground, fall has arrived and snow will start falling soon.

Waterfowl in the millions arrive in Alaska in spring to breed and raise their chicks. Countless lakes and ponds provide food and secure nest sites. The largest and most conspicuous water birds in Denali are the swans. Most of the breeding pairs in the park are tundra swans. The larger trumpeter swan can only be spotted rarely.

Due to poor drainage, low evaporation and a shorter growing season than at lower latitude, small ponds dot the taiga. Most have neither inlet nor outlet. They are maintained by snow melt, rain and run-off from the surrounding terrain. Many are shallow and support little fish life if any. However, they offer perfect conditions for the development of insect eggs and larvae.

The upper slopes turn scarlet as the sun kisses Denali good night. In fall, when darkness reigns again in the small hours of the day, curtains of lights sometimes dance above the mountain. The Aurora borealis is nature's light show. The earth's magnetic field directs electrons from solar eruptions into the upper atmosphere, where they interact with oxygen and nitrogen. To the naked eye, the Aurora mostly appears pale green with a vague purplish band at the bottom. Their full color spectrum only becomes visible during strong displays.

Habitats on the south side of the Alaska Range differ from those north of the divide. Instead of boreal forest spreading along waterways, tall cottonwood trees line rivers and streams at lower elevation. Wildlife sightings commonly involve different species as well. While bald eagles and black bears are both wide-spread north of the mountain range, they do not frequent the open tundra and are seen only rarely in the park. The best odds to see either is along the road corridor heading to Denali from the south. The same holds true for the coyote.

Most rivers originating at glaciers appear half full. However, while their levels rise and fall due to changes in snow melt and rainfall, they are never completely full from bank to bank unless an outburst flood from a glacial lake or Jökulhlaup washes downstream. The braided appearance of the river bed is due to the high amount of sediment in the water. As the material gets deposited where water speed drops, the river channels constantly alter their course.

Steep slopes hem the bubbling creek on both sides. Even during the height of summer, sunlight rarely penetrates into this north facing ravine. Snow lingers on in the shade, the meltwater feeding the tumbling brook. A route barely noticeable among the scree climbs up toward the mountain pass above, crisscrossing the stream several times. Finally the path levels off. My gaze lifts from the ground in front me. Time seems to stand still as I look about, spellbound. There is no slow introduction to the heart of this mountain kingdom, no minor view points to prepare the adventurous backpacker. I stare in disbelief at the peaks, ridges, rock faces and glaciers, all so close that it seems possible to touch yet they are still miles in the distance. The mind fights to attach scale. The world around seems surreal, too large to be true, too big to feel small.

Beyond the pass the terrain falls off steeply to the wide frozen swathe of the Muldrow Glacier below. On the opposite side, hanging glaciers hide the rocky heart of Mount Carpe and Mount Tatum. Just to the east, Mount Brooks towers. To the west, the Muldrow winds upward to huge ice falls. Beyond, Pioneer Ridge guides the gaze toward the South Peak of Denali just over ten miles away. The mountain seems to reach for the sky.

Over a hundred years ago, in late March 1910, the same view greeted four miners from the gold rush town of Kantishna: Tom Lloyd, Pete Anderson, Billy Taylor, and Charles McGonagall, who gave the pass his name. They became known as the Sourdough Expedition. To this day, their accomplishment remains one of the most astounding feats of mountaineering in Alaska. None of them had climbed mountains previously, nor did they continue to scale peaks afterwards. In fact, their famed ascent was born out of a bar bet. At the time, a hotly debated issue in all taverns across the state was the false claim of Dr. Frederick Cook to have summited Denali in 1906. Tom Lloyd argued that no outsider could scale the mountain. However, if anyone could make the climb, there were several pioneers of his acquaintance, him included, who could. The bar owner, Bill McPhee, challenged Lloyd's bold statement and the bet was on. And like so many undertakings arising from the bottom of a beer mug, the Sourdoughs displayed a mixture of resolve, amazing endurance and great skill in wilderness travel in the far north yet also considerable naïvety regarding the core objective of their undertaking: after getting to the base of the mountain, they had to climb to its very top. They were all novice mountaineers with rudimentary, homemade equipment. On the mountain, they used no ropes as "we did not need them". Any climber showing up at base camp today equipped as they were would be accused of being on a suicide mission.

Unburdened by such concerns, the Sourdoughs left Fairbanks in late 1909. By March they had explored a promising approach route and had set up base camp on the upper Muldrow Glacier. And on April 3rd, Charley McGonagall, Pete Anderson and Billy Taylor left their camp at 11,000 feet elevation, carrying a fourteen foot spruce pole, a flag, a bag of doughnuts and a thermos of hot chocolate, heading for the summit. At 19,000 feet

Alpenglow on the north peak of Denali ▲

INTO FORBIDDING HEIGHTS

The granite walls of Moose's Tooth rising above the Ruth Glacier

Denali as seen from Eielson Visitor Center

View from McGonagall Pass

the older McGonagall stayed back behind. His job had been to get the pole within striking distance. That done, there was no reason for him to go any further, he later stated. Anderson and Taylor continued to the summit of the North Peak of Denali and planted the flagpole on a rock outcrop just below its highest point. They never climbed the technically easier but slightly higher south peak as its summit was not visible from nearby Kantishna. The Sourdoughs returned to their base camp in the evening of that day. They still had several doughnuts in their bag. Assisted in their ascent by favorable conditions, the Sourdough party had completed their climb in eighteen hours. Today, modern climbing expeditions with crampons, ice axes, insulated plastic boots and lightweight down

continued on page 60

The Kahiltna Glacier spills down from Denali. The majority of climbers attempting to summit the mountain establish a base camp on the Kahiltna. After ferrying equipment up the glacier and establishing camps ever higher up, they follow the West Buttress Route to the top.

Mount Hunter or Begguya - "the Child" - 14,573 feet (4,442 m) tall, is one of the most challenging peaks to climb in the Alaska Range. There is no easy route, just long, steep and corniced ridges or walls of mixed rock and ice.

The Great Gorge of the Ruth Glacier is about one mile wide. Granite cliffs over 5,000 feet high rise above its crevassed surface. The ice in the Great Gorge is more than 3,500 feet thick. If all were removed, the Grand Canyon would lose its place as the deepest chasm in North America. Many of the spires and vertical cliffs dwarf the famous rock walls of Yosemite. Here, few have been named and many have never been climbed.

Ravens have been seen near the summit of Denali.

The east face of Mount Dickey is one of the tallest rock walls in the world. ▶

Storm clouds hide Moose's Tooth.

parkas commonly spend a week to retrace their route. Their record time has never been repeated, even by people not burdened with a flagpole.

Their mission accomplished, Charles McGonagall, Pete Anderson and Billy Taylor went directly to Kantishna to work their claims in pursuit of their dream of riches. Yet glory for their successful ascent was slow to come. Unfortunately, their flagpole proved to be invisible both from Kantishna and from Fairbanks. In addition, Tom Lloyd, who was the only party member to travel to Fairbanks to announce their feat, embellished his part in the climb. As a result the Sourdough Climb was soon regarded as another tall tale. Their amazing achievement might have never found the recognition it deserves if it wasn't for the

Broken Tooth

The Ruth Glacier has sliced deeply into the surrounding mountains, creating vertical cliffs that are both a climber's nightmare and paradise.

A climbing party searches for a route through a crevasse field.

climbing party of Hudson Stuck three years later. En route to the first ascent of the higher South Peak, all four expedition members spotted the flagstaff from the great basin separating the north and south summits. They were the only people ever to verify its existence. With the mountain conquered, interest faded. The next expedition to climb the North Peak was not until 1932. By then, no evidence of the pole could be found anymore.

In the early climbing days on Denali, all expeditions that were successful or even made it near the summit, had approached from the north. This changed in 1951. After an extensive aerial survey, Bradford Washburn was dropped off by ski plane on the Kahiltna Glacier. He and his party then skied up the Kahiltna, scaled the West Buttress, and continued on to Denali Pass. From there, with all technical difficulties behind them and as conditions were good, the South Peak was but an exposed, high elevation stroll away. Today most summit attempts are made via the route he pioneered.

◀ *Mount Huntington*

Mile 2: Summer deluge over Nenana River Valley

> "*No comfort, no security, no invention, no brilliant thought, which the modern world had to offer, could provide half the elation of the days spent in the little-explored, uninhabited world of the Arctic wilderness.*"

Robert Marshall, Alaska Wilderness

JOURNEY INTO DENALI'S WILD HEART

Mile 3: Fall storm dusting Sugarloaf Mountain

A 91 mile long band of pavement and gravel provides access into the wild heart of Denali National Park. The road's location was a compromise between the Alaska Road Commission and the National Park Service. The ARC was mandated to provide vehicular access to settlements and attempted to establish a "lower" route between the railroad tracks and the mining settlement of Kantishna, located north of the park boundary at the time. The National Park service favoured an "upper" route across high passes, which would terminate near the base of Denali for its scenic values. Funding for both projects was unavailable. In 1923, road work along the upper route commenced. By 1929, the East Fork of the Toklat River was reached. Work on Polychrome Pass began the following year. In 1932, a graded route existed to the location of present day Eielson Visitor Center at mile 66. By the end of the 1936 construction season, Wonder Lake was accessible by vehicle. Finally, in late 1938, Kantishna was linked to the rail line by road. With the completion of the George Parks Highway in 1971 connecting Anchorage with Fairbanks, usage of the park road increased greatly. It became a necessity to limit access for road safety reasons and also to preserve wildlife viewing opportunities. Today, the first 16 miles of the park road are open to the public. The remainder of this narrow corridor can be accessed by vehicle only aboard a bus or with a special access permit.

Mile 0.9: Horseshoe Lake

The tree-line in Denali lies generally at around 3,000 feet. Below that, the boreal forest or Taiga cloaks the land. The dominant trees are the white and black spruce, with the latter occupying wet, organic soil. They are easily recognizable by their stunted growth. In the fall, groves of aspen add color to the forest. Many of the park's established trails traverse this habitat. Among the most common animals to spot are the red squirrel and the grey jay or camp robber. During the summer, moose cows with their new calves frequent the Horseshoe Lake area to feed. Moose often have two calves, which weigh at birth usually between 28 and 35 pounds. They are born between mid-May and early June. For the first few weeks of their lives, the calves are very vulnerable. Unable to outrun a predator, they depend on camouflage and their mother's protection for survival. Grizzlies are the biggest threat. The bears mostly frequent open terrain. However, during the calving time, many prowl the forest in pursuit of prey.

Mile 6: Taiga forest in autumn colors

The lynx is the largest cat in Denali National Park. While not rare, they are elusive and in most years spotted by very few visitors. Their main food source is the snowshoe hare. Hare populations follow a boom and bust pattern over an eight to eleven year cycle, and the lynx numbers follow suit, though with delay. The best chance to spot a lynx is when the hare population has just crashed. Lynx are still plentiful. However, they now broaden their diet and pursue prey in areas they usually do not frequent such as high mountain slopes and open tundra to catch ptarmigan, ground squirrels or even Dall sheep lambs.

Mile 7: Mount Hayes ▲

Mile 9: Denali as seen from the first view point of the mountain

Mile 11: Healy Ridge

At mile 7, the park road starts to climb out of the forest zone and straddles the tree-line to the Savage River. Prime moose habitat spreads to both sides of the road. During the summer and fall, the animals browse here on the leaves of willow, birch and aspen. In fall, when the willow leaves turn bright red, moose bulls start to congregate in this area. They brush the velvet off their palmate antlers. Early in the morning, their mating calls may be heard. They are on the look-out for prospective mates and feed little during this time. The peak of the rut activities is in late September and early October when the leaves long have dropped and temperatures dip below freezing at night. By late October, the males have exhausted their fat reserves and their interest in females fades. The animals head to lower elevations for better winter forage.

Generally, only the largest bulls will breed. A dominant male will have up to a dozen females in his harem and will defend his mating rights against all intruders. Constantly he uses his sense of smell to check whether any of his cows have come into estrus. It is a restless time for the bulls and physically draining. After the rut, they drop their antlers and focus on replenishing their fat reserves for the long winter ahead.

Most confrontations between bulls end without a fight. When a dominant male approaches, smaller bulls avoid conflict and move off. However, if two males of roughly the same size compete over mating rights, fights can get violent and potentially may result in severe injury or death.

Beyond Mile 16, between the Savage and Sanctuary Rivers, Primrose Ridge rises on the north side of the road. Up high, bands of Dall sheep ewes with their lambs and small bachelor groups of rams forage. They rarely come down to lower elevation as they depend on steep terrain for protection. During the summer months, caribou often seek out exposed ridges and slopes as well to avoid various types of biting insects.

Mile 31.2: Teklanika River

The gravel bars of the braided rivers in the park are travel corridors used by many animals. Wolves, grizzlies, moose and caribou are frequently seen. The ground is level and open, making it easy to detect danger. Along the water's edge, a slight breeze keeps the mosquitoes down. The Eskimo Potato blooms along the banks. In the thickets lining the river, soap berries grow profusely. They are a favoured food source of grizzlies, although their flavour, as the name suggests, is an acquired taste. However, the berries are rich in fat and grow in dense clusters, allowing the animals to consume great quantities with little effort.

Mile 34.1: Igloo Creek

High above Igloo Creek, Dall sheep are almost always visible grazing or resting on an alpine slope. Below, along the creek bottom, the forest provides habitat for very different animals, adapted to the shelter of the trees. Many are rarely seen while not uncommon such as the pine marten and the great grey owl. Others like the spruce grouse are conspicuous and easily observed. Blueberries seem to grow everywhere and provide a tasty snack in late summer.

Mile 39.1: View from Sable Pass

The Sable Pass Wildlife Closure extends between Mile 38 and Mile 43. It is the only area within the park permanently closed to hiking for the protection of wildlife. Sable Pass is a hot spot for a number of species. Golden Eagles soar above the steep slopes on the look-out for ground squirrels. Moose bulls feed in willow thickets. Wolves travel through. But most of all, Sable Pass is known for its grizzlies. Bear families are often observed here as they feed, play and rest.

They do not belong to the Big Five. Few will have them on their list of must-see-animals. But they are still an integral part of the ecosystems in Denali. They occupy the lower end of the food chain and without them, many others could not exist. They play an important role in the diet of animals such as foxes, bears and eagles. They are the rodents and hares. Most noticeable of them all are the Arctic ground squirrels. They scurry around every picnic table and inquisitively eye passing vehicles from along the road edge. The hoary marmot is the largest rodent in the park, weighing up to ten pounds and may exceed 24 inches (61 cm) in length. The collared pika is frequently heard before seen. Their unmistakable warning whistle is characteristic in the high alpine areas in Denali. Pikas live in scree slopes where their grey fur blends in perfectly with the rock. They are closely related to hares and in contrast to the ground squirrels and marmots do not hibernate. Their winter survival depends on their success in haymaking during the summer months. All three of them can be found in the Polychrome Pass area (Mile 45.9)

◀ ***Red fox with snowshoe hare***

Mile 48: Murie Plains

As the road winds down from Polychrome Pass, hugs I-Scream-Gulch and then heads along the Toklat River, dead spruce trees line the road. Decades ago, in a severe winter, porcupines were trapped in this small forest by deep snow. To survive, they debarked the trees, killing them. Porcupines seem unlikely denizens on the tundra. However, during the summer, they venture quite far from the boreal forest to nibble on luscious twigs.

Caribou frequent the open tundra between the East Fork River and Thorofare Pass. Newborn calves are rarely seen here as the calving area of the Denali herd lies further to the west in the Kantishna Hills. The calves are born in early June, and start walking within hours of birth. Mortality is high in the first two weeks of their lives. Afterwards they can outrun most predators.

Mile 66: Rain shower drenching the foothills

Denali creates its own weather. During the summer months, many visitors never get to the see the mountain from along the park road. The entire park can be bathed in glorious sunlight, yet Denali hides its head behind clouds. During the day, the sun reflecting off the ice and snow warms up the air above the mountain's steep flanks. As the warm air rises, moist air from the surrounding lowlands rushes in and clouds form. As a consequence, during the early morning hours and late at night, the odds are best to get a glimpse of the summit.

◂ *Mile 62: Denali from Stony Hill Overlook*

Lichens are an important part of tundra and taiga ecosystems. They are a winter food source for caribou. As an organism, lichens are unusual as, in fact, they are a composite consisting of algae living among fungi filaments in a symbiotic relationship. They have no roots and no flowers and are often overlooked. They generally grow very slowly and have a long life-span. Some species are considered to be among the oldest living organisms.

▲ *Mile 66: Tundra at Eielson Visitor Center*

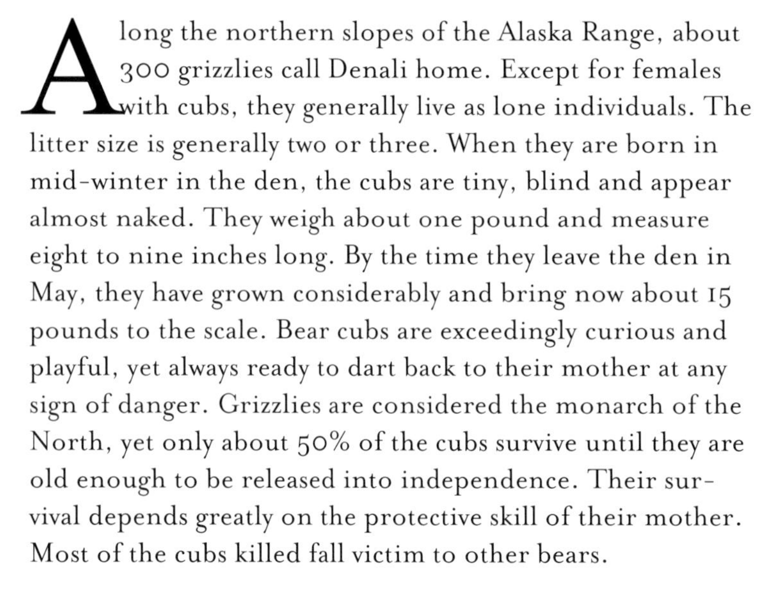

Along the northern slopes of the Alaska Range, about 300 grizzlies call Denali home. Except for females with cubs, they generally live as lone individuals. The litter size is generally two or three. When they are born in mid-winter in the den, the cubs are tiny, blind and appear almost naked. They weigh about one pound and measure eight to nine inches long. By the time they leave the den in May, they have grown considerably and bring now about 15 pounds to the scale. Bear cubs are exceedingly curious and playful, yet always ready to dart back to their mother at any sign of danger. Grizzlies are considered the monarch of the North, yet only about 50% of the cubs survive until they are old enough to be released into independence. Their survival depends greatly on the protective skill of their mother. Most of the cubs killed fall victim to other bears.

Grizzlies are omnivorous. In Denali, their diet consists mostly of plant matter. In spring, they dig for roots and feed on new shoots. In fall, they fatten up on berries. However, bears are the epitome of an opportunist. They will utilize any food source rich in calories. Grizzlies will scavenge the kills of other predators, scan the hillsides for carcasses of animals that died during the winter, prey heavily on newborn moose and caribou calves, and they will bring down injured or sick herbivores such as caribou. They also have a fondness for ground squirrels, excavating their burrows in pursuit of them.

◀ ***Despite its name, the black bearberry is not an important food plant for bears.***

Winter is a time of food shortage for most wildlife and animals have developed different strategies to cope. Most birds migrate south for the cold part of the year. Dall sheep move to mountain slopes that receive little snow. Moose seek out river bottoms with heavy brush for them to browse on during the winter. Wolves follow their prey. Foxes change their hunting strategy. Many rodents stay active underneath the snow. The sly hunter pin points their position with his hearing and pounces onto his unsuspecting victim through the snow cover. Pikas and red squirrels stockpile food during the summer to retrieve and feed on in winter. Some animals wait out the period of hardship fast asleep. They hibernate. Hibernation, however, is not without problems. The animal has to accumulate enough fat reserves to make it through the winter. While asleep they still burn calories. Hibernating ani-

Migrating sandhill cranes in spring ▲

mals are potentially vulnerable to predation as they cannot defend themselves or run away to escape danger. In addition there are physiological problems such as how to avoid muscle atrophy and how to get rid of metabolic waste. The body temperature of Arctic Ground squirrels can drop below freezing during hibernation. Yet the animals still have to wake up regularly to urinate and defecate, eat and drink a bit and then go back to sleep. Bears are too large to follow that pattern. Their body temperature in winter lowers by only six to sixteen degrees Fahrenheit from normal. While they burn more calories because of a higher metabolic rate, they are able to recycle waste products. In addition, this allows the animals to go through pregnancy during hibernation.

Mile 79: A beaver tows a branch to his lodge.

The landscape and ecosystems change west of the Eielson Bluffs. Wet tundra sprawls to both sides of the road covered with willow and blueberry bushes and alder thickets. The road passes many shallow ponds and several small lakes. Moose stand in the water to feed on weeds. Muskrat build their houses in swamps. There are numerous old beaver lodges lining the lakes. Many are unoccupied. A combination of low water levels and cold winters with little snow cover decimated their population and they are slowly bouncing back.

Mile 80: Denali reflecting in tundra pond

Numerous species of waterfowl breed on the tundra ponds and lakes. Geese and swans can be found on any small body of water that is deep enough to protect the nest from predators. The common loon and red-necked grebe, however, nest only on lakes that support fish life such as Wonder Lake. The haunting call of the loon echoing across the water is one of the most distinctive and memorable sounds of the north. In the wetlands around Wonder Lake, Denali's and Alaska's sole representative of the amphibian world, the wood frog, is also easily found.

Mile 87.5: Bull moose along Wonder Lake

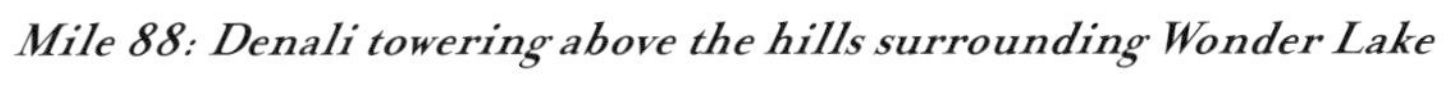

Mile 88: Denali towering above the hills surrounding Wonder Lake

The far end of Wonder Lake offers some of the best views of Denali. The area is also rich in wildlife with moose, caribou and grizzlies utilizing the wealth of food available. The animals can be tough to spot though, hidden in the tall vegetation.

A bull caribou in prime fall condition

DENALI REFLECTION

"We cannot overlook the importance of wild country as source of inspiration, to which we give expression in writing, in poetry, drawing and painting, in mountaineering, or in just being there."

Olaus Murie

Denali reflecting in Wonder Lake still partly covered with ice in early spring.

The shadows are getting longer. Not a single breath of wind mars the surface of the little pond in front of me. A couple of loons float leisurely on the dark water in which the summit of Denali casts a perfect reflection. The sky is clear. It is early fall. Nights are dark again. I hope to photograph star trails reflecting in the lake. A long hike had taken me to this spot. It had taken longer yet to find this secluded place. There is no walking paths or road leading here. I had followed a game trail through the brush. This is my own, private refuge. Just sitting quietly, nature reveals itself to the patient. Moose appear at the lake's edge, lynx on the prowl sneak by quietly. You cannot force yourself upon wilderness. If you do, you will always remain a stranger, a foreign object struggling with the environment. To become a part of your surroundings requires to open up and let them in. Some people recharge batteries at social events, at a party, in a crowd. For a business leader or a politician, the ability to do so might be a requirement. Others, however, me included, need solitude to refuel. For me, wild places where nature, not man, rules are not a luxury but a necessity essential to happiness, to peace of mind, to physical and mental health. Over the years, I have visited many places in Denali that have taken my breath away. In the presence of immense beauty, the question of the meaning of life seems moot. The answer is all around. Each of these precious moments have engraved themselves into memory. They give me comfort, direction, hope and strength when the demands and turmoils of fast modern life seem overwhelming.

The sun has sunk behind the horizon. The upper

Autumn sunrise on Denali

reaches of Denali turn scarlet as if the mountain drinks in the last of the day. As the sunlight fades, colors turn into shades of grey until they too dissolve into blackness and the forest appears stencilled against the night sky. The night lingers in hushed silence. Only on the northern horizon, a vague remembrance of light remains as a narrow band subdued by the darkness above. All of a sudden, misty waves of light drift like pale moon-lit clouds across the star-studded sky. They grow stronger, turn into pale green curtains hemmed below by a thin red ribbon, blown across the firmament by some celestial wind. The lights dance for hours, cast Denali in their spotlight, then almost disappear only to grow stronger again minutes later. Finally the sky above falls quiet again. As I settle down into my sleeping bag and close my eyes, the wail of a loon reverberates across the lake. Denali bestows parting gifts that keep on giving.

The midnight sun illuminating clouds above the taiga forest.

Published by

BreiterView Publishing
11 Snow Place
Kenora, Ontario P9N OE6
Canada
email: matthias.breiter@breiterphoto.com
www.breiterphoto.com

Printed in Canada

Editor: Eric Matheson, Kenora, Ontario; Laurel Snyder, Kenora, Ontario
Design: Matthias Breiter

ISBN: 978-0-9782432-5-8

The pages of this book were printed on chlorine free paper made with 10% post-consumer waste, saving 6 fully grown trees, 2,677 gallons of water, 163 pounds of solid waste and 556 pounds of greenhouse gases.